IF..., THEN...

The Power of Risk Management for Busy People with Other Things to Do

Tom O'Connor

authorHOUSE®

AuthorHouse™
1663 Liberty Drive
Bloomington, IN 47403
www.authorhouse.com
Phone: 1-800-839-8640

Published by AuthorHouse   10/29/2014

ISBN: 978-1-4969-4969-1 (sc)
ISBN: 978-1-4969-4968-4 (e)

Library of Congress Control Number: 2014919313

To those who prefer to avoid problems rather than spending valuable time and resources just to get back to where you had been.

Preface

This book is based upon the one singular belief that the discipline of comprehensive risk management can bring tangible bottom-line benefits to owners, executives, and managers who haven't previously given it much thought.

This belief shatters some time-tested conventional wisdom while guiding you to success in managing your risks, specifically the following:

1. *A common consulting technique is to employ some assessment or other diagnostic tool to convince the client that additional products and services are required to reach the stated goal.*
  - As a veteran of forty years of consulting as an employee of large, well-known firms, I am fully aware of this tactic. But, quite frankly, I'm old enough to want to avoid returning to the life of a road warrior at this stage of my life.
  - This book will guide you to independence and self-sufficiency in managing your own risks and, it will accomplish this during the first experience with the process as long as you pay attention. No additional products are needed; any additional services should be minimal or totally unnecessary.
2. *Consultants must come with experience and insights into your industry to be worth their fees.*
  In many instances, this is correct, but there are also instances where the consultant and/or the tool can effectively facilitate drawing on your insights to create actionable information. This is one of those instances.
3. *Risk management requires high cost and commitment in terms of money and time and also requires lots of specialized expertise.*
  None of these are true. This approach has been deliberately designed to lead working managers to

effective results. That is what "designed for busy people with other things to do" means.

4. *And finally, consultants bearing gifts are cause for caution.* I will not violate the trust I want to earn.

I encourage you to read about this straightforward and economical approach to open the door to new opportunities and fewer setbacks.

Tom

Introduction

Traveling through a Tough Neighborhood

blog.sms-ga.com, December 2012

What do you do when you find yourself traveling through a tough neighborhood at night? It is probably second nature that you become more alert and focused. You pay more attention to your peripheral vision and listen for unusual sounds. You might even run through stop signs and traffic lights if you sense that danger is close. These responses are not instinctive, though they may now seem so. You learned that these actions are the prudent thing to do in these situations to protect yourself and those who are important to you.

Can anyone question that running a goal-oriented enterprise (business, nonprofit, volunteer, government) is a continuous journey through a tough neighborhood? Lots of things can go wrong; and when they do, they slow or even halt your progress toward your goals. This book guides you in learning how to protect the progress of your professional responsibilities in this tough, unforgiving world.

This book will introduce you to the Protect-Biz risk management planning process. This process is designed for busy people who have other things to do. Moreover, it is designed to lead you to independence and self-sufficiency in the critical discipline of risk management. The process is straightforward, sophisticated, and very powerful. Its power will be demonstrated through examples and simple exercises that will address your world of risks.

The first time through the process, you will learn exponentially—about your risks and also about how to protect against the damages they can cause. You will also learn how to use this approach for the remainder of your life, as it will become second nature. And the best thing about it becoming second nature is that future use of the process is totally free of charge for those new risks that come with newfound achievement and success.

This is the value the Protect-Biz risk management planning process offers. It is unique and direct. And while it is the risk management tool specifically created for busy people who have other things to do, commitment and thought are required for identifying, avoiding, and anticipating risks to your success. These are not tasks to completely delegate to others. Would a pilot delegate all preflight checks to the mechanics?

Focusing on what could go wrong in the future might seem like a negative thing to do. But actually, risk management offers much more than the prevention of pain and expense; it offers an uninterrupted focus on growth and success. It opens doors to opportunities you might not have considered or planned. And it offers fulfillment of your goals and your dreams. Risk management is the management discipline that unlocks new possibilities.

Do you lock your doors at night? If you do, you are already practicing risk management. Do you acknowledge that your competitive position is always at risk? What you do with that thought is an example of how risk management can drive you to innovation and opportunities.

The remainder of this book will guide you in dramatically harnessing the power of risk management to achieve your goals reliably, with lower costs, and in shorter time frames.

Table of Contents

List of Examples

1. What Is Risk Management?

Risk without Risk Management—A Small Biz Case Study

blog.sms-ga.com, November 2013

A friend and colleague owns businesses in three locations within the United States. I do not know the exact size of each, but I'll guess they are in the small to midsized category. He is a capable manager and probably assumes he can handle whatever comes up.

Now let us refer to these three locations as A, B, and C. He and his family reside near one of them. He divides his time between the three locations on a regular basis. And his business has recently experienced an unexpected upsurge in business.

Very recently, one of his distant key employees suffered a disabling injury due to an accident and will be unable to work for two to three months. This prompted immediate travel to this other location with the parting words, "I'll be there for two to three months." This seems like a reasonable and necessary response. But it is also where the informal, subconscious approach to risk management falls apart.

Now his planned task list is turned upside down. His other two locations are without his attention and help, his employees may be confused about their authority and priorities in his absence, and his overall business may suffer as a result until he can get everything put back together as a smoothly running organization—in other words, the ingredients for a setback with bottom-line implications.

There is an alternative to such an informal, seat-of-the-pants approach to risk management. It can lead you to preplanned responses instead of quickly conceived reactions born under a sense of urgency. It can help you see beyond the immediate issue and address the implications that ripple through the rest of the organization. It also communicates your planned response and the secondary ramifications of your response to others in the organization—the people who make it run. And all of this can be accomplished in a planning mode, not a crisis mode.

An often overlooked step in the planning process ...

As a person with significant professional responsibilities, you probably worry about things that might go wrong. But worrying is not a productive activity. To turn unproductive worries into productive action, planning is the necessary ingredient to put those worries to productive use.

The act of planning is ubiquitous even though lots of planning never gets recorded on paper or in a computer file. You surely have visions of the future, near and far, and strive to achieve them. The typical planning process starts with the desired objective and then identifies the steps to achieve it.

But these steps don't always unfold the way you want them to. You know that, but you frequently bypass the part of the planning process that could help prevent you from being caught flat-footed and asking the question, "What might go wrong?" This is the starting point for risk management. It is the starting point for you to protect your plans and activate your ability to achieve your goals and objectives on time and within budget.

So if you acknowledge that an extra step in the planning process might save your plans from delays, added expense, and maybe even abandonment, what do you do next?

Well, you can start wondering about how the rest of the professional world employs risk management. And here is where it can get a little confusing if you are not clear in what you may be looking for.

Risk management shows signs of an identity crisis ...

Once you start to look for it, risk management can be found in lots of places. A simple Internet search demonstrates that there is no shortage of opinions, specialized expertise, recommended credentials, and international standards and sophisticated and expensive tools available. But a closer look reveals a critical fact:

> *The banner of risk management is carried by many different professions with differing meanings.*

They are not all referring to the same range of risks or even what to do about them. So the first words to the wise are "One size does not fit all."

The Risk Management Elephant

blog.sms-ga.com, October 2013

Many of us have heard the parable of blind men each touching a different part of an elephant but not being able to reconcile their individual findings to determine what it really is. It seems that risk management presents a modern example of this challenge, albeit with a twist. Here, instead of blindfolds, we are wearing blinders that restrict the breadth of our vision.

In this case, recognition that the part of the "critter" we see is risk management is not the problem. Rather, it is in comprehending that other parts of the animal are risk management too.

Even at the most basic foundation of embracing risk management as a valuable management tool ("Why do this?"), the viewpoints can quickly diverge. There are those who see risk management as being about the transfer of risk (i.e., insurance); for others, it is about diversification. Then there are those focused on regulatory compliance, while others still try to satisfy governance requirements that can vary widely. Moreover, let us not forget those applying risk management while evaluating opportunities (e.g., mergers and acquisitions, new ventures) or those just trying to improve their ability to achieve their goals.

Each of these people can easily and correctly declare that his or her piece is risk management. But accepting that other entirely different portions of the elephant are also risk management is not always easy to reconcile into a single explanation, for each of these viewpoints brings its own reference by which to measure success, as well as its own particular focus with respect to the specific things to consider, include, avoid, detect, and mitigate.

On top of these differences is another whole dimension to this challenge—what I call my version of the risk management maturity curve. There are those who don't necessarily acknowledge risks as anything other than just a part of the cost of doing business (e.g., risk transfer, diversification, basic physical and cyber security, solving problems so they hopefully will not happen again). Let us call that **Level 1**.

Level 2 moves a step further, with a conscious acknowledgment of the value of risk management as a tool, but it is not yet a budget line item, because it is "part of every manager's job." This represents the first step in the critical concept of moving risks from hindsight into foresight.

Level 3 represents a big step, because it opens the door to risk management specialists, a defined and robust infrastructure, and one or more budget line items. It also includes the concept of risk management standards (e.g., ISO 31000).

An additional dimension of the enterprise can insert risk management expectations into the relationships with external partners, such as suppliers and distributors. Whew! All of this as well as the unique elements of the organization's culture must still be carefully considered before the path to success is clear.

"So what?" you might ask. Well, I suggest that an understanding of so many diverse perspectives of this one topic is a major challenge unto itself. Comprehending this can help facilitate both an improved common understanding and also more effective discussions that lead to actionable outcomes. Think of trying to explain risk management to your board of directors.

Once you comprehend the fact that the risk management banner carried by an insurance agent is not the same as the banner carried by a compliance officer in a bank or the COO of a manufacturing company, you can become more specific in your research to address your own particular needs.

But the fact remains that if you are looking for guidance in addressing a broad definition of risk management, the search results can still be intimidating. The sirens of international standards, infrastructure, specialists, the needs of governance, and some confusing terminology can easily lead you to the conclusion that the commitment is just too great to venture beyond what you may already be doing. This expense and complexity is *not required* for getting tangible results from the fundamentals of risk management offered by the Protect-Biz risk management planning process.

This book is about getting started with risk management:

- without specialists (long term);
- with minimal infrastructure;
- without international standards;
- using simple terminology; and
- at minimal cost and commitment
- while on a very short path to achieving self-sufficiency and independence in managing your own risks

The straightforward mantra "Identify, avoid, anticipate, and get back to work" is our beacon. But what is even more basic than the "Identify, avoid, and anticipate" mantra? It is foresight—creating the foresight that allows you to avoid learning the hard way through painful and costly hindsight. This is the essence and goal of risk management.

IF..., *THEN...* is all about moving risks from hindsight into foresight. With foresight, you will have more time to prevent risks from causing setbacks for your business— and if you cannot avoid them, you can anticipate them with preplanned responses. With foresight, your actions and responses are rooted in planning, not urgency and crisis.

No specialists?

The Protect-Biz risk management planning process encourages you to start small and simple. But why not with the long-term help of specialists? If, for example, you seriously considered the possibility that a key supplier would file for bankruptcy, would you know what to do to:

- position your business to better handle the possibility?
- see it coming?
- respond quickly and decisively to minimize the impact?

Of course you would. So you don't need much specialized expertise to get that far.

Less infrastructure rather than more

The need for infrastructure is dependent upon the size of your business. But start small, and only add what you need.

Risk management should remain a means to an end (goal accomplishment) rather than an end in and of itself.

Is there a need to go chasing after competing international standards that are not certifiable? Maybe, but certainly not before you have received any benefits from the basic process.

As for terminology ...

Which do you prefer:

1. Risk is any potential obstacle between you and your goals (Protect-Biz); or
2. Risk is the effect of uncertainty on an objective (ISO 31000)?

You decide—which definition leads you to a direct plan of action or is even repeatable by separate assessments?

Or how about wrestling with the term *risk appetite*? While it can be useful in making decisions, the implication that you have a control knob that allows you to dial up the amount of risk you are willing to accept does not apply to the myriad of risks just waiting to turn your production schedule upside down.

As for cost ...

The approach described in this book estimates that the people who make direct contribution to your risk management plan commit between five and ten dedicated hours to creating the initial plan and then thirty minutes to an hour each month to reviewing and maintaining it. The size of your business will determine the number of people who need to be involved. As an example, we estimate that a company of two to fifty employees may require one or two people to create and manage the risk management plan.

Using this economical process to create foresight will avoid and minimize the surprises that can negatively impact your business. This represents bottom-line value. Moreover, it can create even more value as described in the next chapter.

2. Benefits

During World War II, then general Dwight D. Eisenhower said, "When preparing for battle, I have found plans to be useless, but planning to be indispensable." Here are many of the ways risk management planning is indispensable.

As stated earlier, risk management is a means to an end, not an end in and of itself. Thus, it must provide tangible benefits to earn a respected place in the manager's tool kit. Tough-minded managers rightfully expect nothing less. Some of the benefits have been stated already, but some have not. Some may surprise you, for they all help change unplanned reactions conceived in moments of urgency into thoughtfully planned responses.

Foresight instead of hindsight

Experience is the teacher of all things.

—Julius Caesar

Experience, the Tardy Professor
blog.sms-ga.com, April 2013

We all have metaphorical people who speak to us within our minds. Our conscience is one of them. And there are others. Each of us has our very own professor of experience, and he or she is one of the additional voices.

Our professor of experience is our personal and primary teacher once we leave the confines of structured schooling. If we pay attention, our professor of experience can teach us things across an infinite range of subjects.

But everyone's professor of experience has one fundamental shortcoming—he or she always misses the first opportunity to guide us to do things right. Thus, it would seem we are destined to make mistakes at least once and therefore sentenced to dwell in the Land of Hindsight for many of our learning experiences.

What kinds of mistakes? All kinds. Ignoring changes in the market; allowing supplier prices to increase unnoticed; cash flow shortfalls; public relations gaffes; security breaches; rework; callbacks; misplaced trust in others; being blindsided by employee/tenant/customer/patient/client defections. You name it—anything can disrupt progress toward your goals.

It is well accepted that hindsight is twenty-twenty. Hindsight is the reference material for our professor of experience. Make no mistake; this is valuable material from which to learn. But it can be costly and painful, sometimes even beyond pain, in that first experience.

The question becomes, "Can we get this learning opportunity to somehow show up prior to that first painful experience? Can we get our professor of experience to show up early? In other words, can we move from the Land of Hindsight to the Land of Foresight?" Considering this is all in the metaphorical regions of our minds, we may have some ability to do just that. This mental projection into the future a primary function of risk management.

Just as athletes train with mental visualization, just as astronauts and pilots train with simulators, risk management disciplines allow us to craft similar mental processes to peer into the future and change that future for the benefit of our businesses. This can save lots of expense and pain and even open doors for much more added value. These proactive prevention and preparation steps are basic elements of any complete risk management approach.

An extended view into the future

As a business owner or executive, how valuable would it be if you could look into the future? Chances are that it would be invaluable. You would be able to better anticipate market changes, see risks before they happen, and better adapt to business growth. You could also see opportunities and have more time to take better advantage of them.

The Protect-Biz risk management planning process extends your vision into the future. Defining risk as "any potential obstacle between you and your goals" forces you to look beyond the here and now. Additionally, the required definition of trip wires and the designation of trip wire monitors guide the organization to a high level of vigilance for detecting real problems that may start small and grow gradually. Far from a useless exercise, confronting and answering questions about future possibilities moves valid risks into the light of day and into foresight, where they can be avoided and effectively mitigated.

Cost reduction—avoid time and expense just to get back to where you have been

---

Ounces More Valuable Than Pounds
blog.sms-ga.com, September 2013

Many of us know the old adage "An ounce of prevention is worth a pound of cure." It teaches us the relatively high value and low cost of prevention over the high cost and low added value of a cure.

But what about prevention's siblings, planning and preparation? I'm sure we can all recall circumstances where the benefits of planning would have outweighed the costs of little or no planning. And is lack of preparation any different?

Prevention, planning, and preparation—these siblings, born by the managerial arts, are all about cost avoidance. These costs can be measured in terms of the limited resources of money, time, energy, and lost opportunities, albeit more easily after the fact when we did not avoid the costs. Combined, they just might represent three ounces of management that are worth at least three pounds of the unnecessary costs of a cure.

This alliteration of business management tasks is also known by an easier term: risk management. Have you figured out what all this talk of risk management is all about? Stick with us, and we will explain it to you in simple and straightforward terms. And we won't break your bank to let you experience its power.

How many times have you been surprised by an event that cost unplanned time and money? While the direct costs are easy to tabulate after the fact, many of the total costs can be as hidden as the bottom of an iceberg. Lost opportunities, distracted attention, rearranged priorities, and the inevitable need to "rob Peter to pay Paul" when resources need to be reassigned just to get back to where you have been can be very costly. Moreover, you rarely go back to account for all of these costs once the problem is behind you. So it gets recorded as just the cost of doing business.

But many of these costs become unnecessary when potential obstacles are brought into the light of day and stored in foresight. As a ship's captain and an aircraft's pilot benefit from longer-range radar, you can benefit from an extended vision into the future. Those potential obstacles can be identified and avoided or minimized by some advance planning. This is what risk management planning can do for your enterprise.

Built around a strong bias for action, not paralysis by analysis

The art of worrying is a common malady in today's world quite simply because things can go wrong. However, worrying is not productive if the process merely generates a lengthening list of things to worry about. Alternatively, these worries can be written down and confronted with two simple questions: 1) "How can I avoid this?" and 2) "How can I reduce the impact of this?" Now this leads to actions that will save time and money and even illuminate new opportunities. This is transforming worry into positive and productive steps to improve your chances of achieving your goals. This bias for action is embedded within the Protect-Biz risk management planning process.

There are many approaches to risk management available. I challenge you to compare them on this criterion—bias for constructive action. If you are committed to risk management as a means to goal achievement, a strong bias for constructive action is critical. The alternative is a process that can be long on costs but short on constructive results.

Designed for busy people with other things to do

This process facilitates institutionalizing risk management as a part of every decision maker's job.

Risk management cannot and should not be delegated off of the desk of any individual with the responsibility for goal achievement and success. Thus, risk management is a line, not a staff function. Back to the comment about aircraft pilots—they don't delegate a preflight checklist to a staff function that will remain on the ground. There is a reason for that.

But the fact remains that the people with these responsibilities are very busy people. Asking you to add risk management responsibilities to your extensive list of things to do might be problematic. This is why the Protect-Biz risk management planning process was designed with you in mind. This process will cause basic but critical questions to become second nature:

- "What might go wrong?"
- "What do I/we assume will go right?"
  (These are risks too.)
- "Can we take action to avoid each possibility?"
- "How can we recognize them if they start small?"
- "Who is in the best position to see this happening?"
- "What actions should we take if any of these occur?"
- "Who should have the authority to take these actions?"

Are these questions too burdensome? Actually, I suspect you'll agree that they are critical to effective management at any level.

Protect-Biz Plan Format

Assumptions	Risks	Avoidance	Trip Wires	Trip Wire Monitors	Actions To Mitigate	Authority To Mitigate

Even the copyrighted format of the Protect-Biz risk management plan adds value as it facilitates easy use and maintenance. There is no large document that will sit on a shelf and collect dust. The plan is a straightforward document that can easily be reviewed and updated—no boilerplate, no executive summary, and all text is action oriented. It is as simple as that—simple and powerful.

A shortcut to defining policies and procedures

Have you gotten around to documenting how you want the business to operate? This becomes more important as the business grows, with new people performing tasks that are new to them while the attention of more experienced employees is directed to new responsibilities supporting the growth. But at a time when everyone is busy and the company is in transition, a concentrated effort to document policies and procedures often winds up at the bottom of the priority list.

A risk management planning process undertaken for all of these other reasons and benefits will actually produce a plan that reflects deliberate decisions regarding business operations. The risk management plan will define actions for avoiding and minimizing setbacks, and that is not very far from the basic purpose of documented policies and procedures for the operation of the company. In this case, version 1 of the policies and procedures document can be a free by-product of the risk management planning process.

Transform teams into Teams

Forces That Transform Teams into *Teams*
blog.sms-ga.com, June 2013

There is a big difference between a team and a Team. Teams achieve results; teams go through the motions. Examples are very easy to find. But what causes the difference?

The four stages necessary to achieve a high-performing Team—forming, storming, norming, and performing—are fairly well known and documented. However, there is one essential ingredient that is not obvious from the four stages. And that ingredient is purpose.

A common purpose serves as the raison d'être for the Team. It must be clear and imperative. If the members buy in to the purpose, the team has a much better chance of success than if they don't. The purpose can be winning the World Series, the NBA Championship, or the Super Bowl. But those don't apply to most of us.

However, there are many such causes that do apply to most of us—raising money for a charity, organizing a special event, or even winning the prize in our bowling league are all possibilities. But I am offering one that doesn't necessarily come to mind—*defending against shared risks*. Think of the wagon trains in the nineteenth century. When they were attacked, total strangers formed a Team to accomplish their very survival.

Why is this relevant today? I see many examples of teams struggling without a common purpose the members have embraced. Governing boards offer many of these examples. How many times have you seen such boards disintegrate into separate agendas while shared risks turn malignant in the face of a team that cannot work together?

A risk management workshop, where shared risks are recognized, discussed, and addressed can be an effective way to transform the board (team) into a Team.

Independence and self-sufficiency

As you learned at the beginning of this book ("Traveling through a Tough Neighborhood"), the ability to effectively manage risks is a learned skill. The Protect-Biz risk management planning process guides you through the eight steps necessary to create a comprehensive risk management plan. The learning is forever. The goal is risk management independence and self-sufficiency. The expectation is that this is achieved as a by-product of the process to create your first risk management plan. Unlike some diagnostic tools on the market, there are no additional services or tools that become necessary. While some consulting advice may seem appropriate at times, our expectations are that you will incur a one-time cost that produces long-term benefits. This valuable discipline will become part of your management tool kit for the rest of your life.

Manage more risks effectively

Management by exception is a cornerstone of modern management culture. Reducing long lists to short, manageable ones is a common mode of operation. Questions like "What are our top three (or five) risks?" rule the executive suite. Never mind that there are many more possible obstacles that may come between you and the goals of your organization.

What about the rest of them? To leave them off of the list means that they might surprise you as if you had not thought of them at all. This seems like the wrong response to a valid concern—how to effectively manage a long list of possibilities.

Seventy-Two, Thirteen, Sixty-Four: A Risk Management Case Study

blog.sms-ga.com, February 2014

As the author of the Protect-Biz risk management process, I am always looking for an opportunity to apply this unique brand of risk management to real-world challenges. In this case, I am both the facilitator of and a principle player in the development of a risk management plan for my current responsibility—a sixty-three-thousand-square-foot commercial office building.

When a longtime friend and client asked me to fill in as an interim building manager, I accepted the challenge. My responsibilities include marketing, maintenance, financials, and, of course, tenant satisfaction—the risk side as well as the opportunity side of the equation for a successful enterprise of this type. I have been on the job for two and a half months at this point.

The Protect-Biz risk management process is first and foremost a process for identifying, avoiding, and anticipating risks. Moreover, it offers a fast way to ensure that the owners and the building manager are all on the same page with respect to all of the possible circumstances that may arise—circumstances that may require immediate decisions, potential circumstances that can keep the owners awake at night.

Seventy-two is the number of risks identified during the first step of the Protect-Biz process. These risks span many possibilities, such as a suspicious package found unattended in the building, a toxic spill on the property, an accident resulting in injury on the property, unexpected high-cost corrective maintenance, and death or disability of the building manager, just to name a few of the seventy-two items.

Protect-Biz includes a unique twist to help ensure that a more complete list of risks is identified. In this case, steps 2 and 3 of the process yielded an additional thirteen line items to be addressed by the resulting risk management plan. Thus, we have a list of eighty-five risks to address. While this may represent an unmanageable number in many risk management planning models, this large number is easily managed in the Protect-Biz process.

The next step of the process is the risk avoidance step. Here we identified actions to eliminate or reduce the possibility of these risks ever turning toxic on us—or, if not complete avoidance, then reducing the potential impact. This step can also yield new opportunities previously unrecognized, such as new marketing differentiators. This step yielded opportunities to avoid, reduce, or take greater advantage of sixty-four of these eighty-five line items.

This represents where we are currently in the eight-step Protect-Biz risk management process. Subsequent steps will guide us in defining specific criteria to identify gradual degradations (slide instead of a crash), delegated responsibility for monitoring these criteria, preplanned mitigation actions, and finally, specific delegated authority to initiate the mitigation actions.

How would you like to have such a pragmatic plan for your business? Would it help ensure that you and your team are all on the same page? Are you aware of any other robust risk management process that can document this content for eighty-five risk line items on about nine or ten pages that allow for easy review and update?

There is no need to arbitrarily reduce the list of eighty-five to the top three (or five or ten). The Protect-Biz risk management planning process facilitates prudent and efficient management of all eighty-five.

Risk management and the Protect-Biz risk management planning process in particular offer a long list of tangible benefits—benefits that enhance the bottom line, build a stronger foundation for the future, and help build a culture of Teamwork with a capital *T*—all of this from a few hours of serious planning and a one-time cost for long-term benefits.

3. How to Identify

A wise man puts all his eggs in one basket ... and watches the basket.

— Andrew Carnegie, twentieth-century industrialist

Chapters 3–7 are devoted to explaining the steps of the Protect-Biz risk management planning process. Examples and exercises are included to give you an ability to follow the steps of the process and create a risk management plan.

This chapter will explain how to get started by identifying and documenting risks (potential obstacles between you and your goals). Chapter 4 will explain our position on probability (of occurrence) and impact estimates. Chapter 5 will explain risk avoidance. Chapters 6 and 7 will address how to anticipate these potential obstacles, specifically how to detect them and then how to respond to them.

First, it is important to reiterate that the Protect-Biz risk management planning process can be applied to any risk management circumstance. It is generic in that it makes no assumptions regarding how the risks will be managed (e.g., risk transfer, go/no-go decisions, risk avoidance, risk mitigation, etc). It also does not contain any assumptions regarding whether the risks are related to a specific project, initiative, or continuing business operations. And lastly, Protect-Biz risk management planning process makes no assumptions regarding for-profit, nonprofit, government, or volunteer enterprises. Even personal goals and objectives can gain value from this risk management planning process.

The obvious first step in developing a risk management plan is to identify the risks. In the Protect-Biz risk management planning process, these risks are events that would create obstacles between you and your goals.

Definition: Risk
Any potential obstacle between you or the enterprise and goals.

Your goals may be documented or not. They may be implied or even intuitive, but they are the starting point for identifying risks. The goals may be opening a new business location, launching a new product, maintaining an enterprise that is financially strong, maintaining a high-quality reputation, reaching specified production goals, making the final decision on a business acquisition, or even getting your mother-in-law successfully moved into an assisted-living arrangement.

For each and every goal, the basic question to ask is, "What might go wrong?" This is approached as any brainstorming exercise—try to generate a long list, not a short one, for there will be an opportunity to eliminate risks that are too far "out of the box." But don't be critical too soon. It is all too common that people go through a risk management process and wind up being blindsided anyway. Resist the urge to keep the list short. The objective of this step of the process is to move as many possibilities as possible into foresight. Do not worry about overload.

Some examples may be helpful.

- A large, multinational company was facing a critical, multiyear internal project with an immovable deadline. It had a comprehensive project plan and a dedicated team of fifteen people ensuring that the plan was executed as scheduled. On their first pass of the risks, they identified fifty-four, one of which was the possibility that one or more team members would leave the company before the project was completed.

- A small CPA firm identified twenty-one risks to its business. One of these risks was the possibility that their Internet service provider would experience an extended outage during tax preparation season.
- A commercial office building manager identified ninety-three risks to the goal of maintaining a financially successful enterprise. One of the risks identified was the possibility of a toxic spill on the premises.
- Other possible risks include the following:
  - Print advertiser—client content not acceptable to advertiser
  - Any enterprise—act of nature disrupts operations
  - Business services firm—client refuses to accept product or deliverable
  - Franchise owner—franchisor experiences a public relations problem
  - Land developer—difficulties with the zoning board
  - Manufacturer—changes to regulatory requirements
  - Natural resource exploration and production—unilateral contract terms with government or owner
  - Nonprofit—demand exceeds capacity to serve
  - Start-up—conflict over intellectual property
  - Volunteer organization—loss of critical expertise

As you can see, the process for filling foresight with possible experiences that easily could be found in hindsight is wide ranging.

Exercise #1: Select one to three of your professional goals; identify and write down at least three possible events that could delay or even stop you from achieving the goal(s).

(Stop! Do it! This book is about value to you.)

Congratulations on taking the first step toward improving your ability to achieve your goals as planned! While the rest of the process is not necessarily easy, this book will continue to guide you toward mastery of this valuable discipline.

You are not yet finished with the task of identifying risks. The fact is that some of your ego was possibly involved in the answer to the question, "What might go wrong?" This is because your ego is directly connected to the project or the enterprise you have created. So there is a little voice that tells you, "What do you mean 'risks'? There are not any risks, because I created this!" This little voice is in all of us. We just need to trick it to allow us to get the most complete list we can get.

Definition: Assumptions
Answers to the question, "What do I/we expect to go right?"

The trick is to now ask for assumptions; in other words, "What do we expect to go right?" Assumptions don't carry the stigma that risks carry. It is okay to make assumptions. Thus, if you assume that your client has the ability to pay your invoice, that is not necessarily a planning failure on your part. However, it might not turn out to be true. Remember, we are trying to protect your plans and your enterprise. So in this case, you are going to simply reword your assumption into a risk—the client may not have the ability to pay our invoice (all assumptions can easily be reworded into risks). Now this has become another risk to add to your list. Sometimes this little trick actually causes our initial list of risks to significantly increase, even double.

Here are some examples of assumptions:

- Uninterrupted access to our business locations
- Tax laws and regulations will not change

- Key personnel will not experience a disabling accident
- Mail service will not be interrupted
- Shipping costs will continue to be stable and predictable
- Client's organization supports the project
- Our water supply is uninterrupted
- The public accepts that contraband must be prohibited in schools
- Market expectations are positive
- Customer buying decisions will remain consistent
- The green movement will not affect this industry
- We have high confidence in the demographic data
- Oil and gas are freely tradable
- Board governance is active
- Established grants will be paid on a reliable schedule

While all of these are reasonable assumptions, most certainly any of them may turn out to be false in any particular circumstance. If you can transform these to risks and place the possibilities into your foresight, you will enhance the protection of your plans and goals.

> **Exercise #2:** Identify and write down at least two assumptions related to the goals selected in Exercise #1. Restate these assumptions as risks, and add them to your list.

(Stop! Do it!)

You have now learned the basic methods for identifying risks. You may have other methods, and these can be used too. The objective is to create as long a list as possible, since you don't want to be blindsided one day because you rushed through the risk identification step. But there is no need to agonize over this step. You will always have the opportunity to add risks even after the initial plan is completed.

4. Probability and Impact

Out of clutter, find simplicity.

—Albert Einstein

At this stage of many risk management planning processes, each risk is analyzed in terms of the following: 1) the probability of occurrence, and 2) the potential impact in terms of severity and cost. The Protect-Biz risk management planning process allows for these steps but in most circumstances does not recommend them. And if they might be important, it is recommended that they be deferred until the remainder of the Protect-Biz risk management planning process is completed.

The common rationale for including these steps is back to the management-by-exception rule. Invariably, management will want to draw a line at some arbitrary place on the list of risks—say, 65 percent probability or some similar arbitrary value of potential impact—and proceed to ignore those risks below the line. The reasons we recommend against this are numerous.

1. Being estimates, the probability and the estimated impacts are not exact and can have a large degree of error. While specific numbers may give the impression that they are exact, they are not. This leads to a false sense of security.
2. If the risks listed below the arbitrary cutoff are indeed valid possibilities, they could still blindside the enterprise as if there had been no risk management planning at all.
3. The process of calculating these estimates can severely slow the progress to your goal—the creation

of a plan that specifies actions to avoid, anticipate, and respond to the risks.

4. While the management-by-exception rule assumes that a long list of risks cannot be effectively managed, this is not true with the format of the Protect-Biz risk management plan.

5. And finally, the analysis of these characteristics would typically require specialists who can cause the entire process to fall back into the complicated realm that is clearly outside the world of risk management for busy people with other things to do.

If these analyses and calculations are important in a few circumstances, it is recommended that they be the exceptions rather than the rule. An example is an enterprise with multiple locations near the Gulf and Atlantic coasts of the United States. If the risk of hurricanes requires that materials and recovery personnel be staged in positions to allow a fast response to a hurricane that might impact either coast, then by all means, do this analysis and decide where to stage these resources. We do believe it is also true that the subsequent steps of the Protect-Biz risk management planning process will add valuable information to such analyses. That is why we recommend they be deferred so as not to stop progress through these other critical steps.

5. How to Avoid

Case Study

Our office building is four stories tall and the largest office building in the county. The building is located across the street from a federal courthouse. In this day and age, it does not take much of an imagination to think of what an active shooter could accomplish from our rooftop. But in the forty-two years this building has been here, no one has thought to lock the doors to the roof! Certainly, all active-shooter events are a total surprise. However, a simple precaution like this was identified by the Protect-Biz risk management planning process and serves as an excellent example of the old adage "An ounce of prevention is worth a pound of cure."

Now that you have completed your first iteration through the identify steps, it is time to consider the avoidance step. The avoidance step is focused on repositioning your enterprise to either avoid the possibility of encountering the obstacle entirely or repositioning to reduce the probability of an occurrence or the impact. This is done while the risk is still a possibility rather than a reality.

Definition: Actions to Avoid
Actions to be taken to reposition the enterprise to either avoid the risk altogether or to reduce either the severity of the obstacle or the probability of the risk becoming real.

Think of two ships approaching each other on the high seas. With the advantage of long-range radar over binoculars, the ships may determine that an adjustment in their courses or speeds may significantly reduce the possibility of a collision. This would not, however, be cause to eliminate the risk of collision from their list of risks.

Case Study

Recall the earlier example of a small CPA firm recognizing the possibility of their Internet service provider experiencing an outage that could disrupt their ability to complete tasks for their clients under tight deadlines. In this case, they decided to have a different Internet service provider at their homes to allow a relatively easy and inexpensive shift to working from home if this need arose. In this case, they decided to remove the risk from their list.

Note that in both cases, the action to avoid the risk would not change or cancel the goal. The avoidance step is not intended to change the goal but only to reposition the enterprise to avoid or significantly reduce the possibility of the obstacle becoming real and impacting the ability to reach the goal.

The avoidance step is the only optional step in the Protect-Biz risk management planning process. There may very well be potential obstacles that defy any amount of repositioning. In other words, once a risk is on the list, each subsequent step of the process is required to have a documented response except for the avoidance step. In the commercial building example described earlier, the initial plan included seventy-two risks and thirteen assumptions that added risks for a total of eighty-five risks. That plan also included avoidance actions for sixty-four of the risks—for twenty-one of the eighty-five risks, no avoidance actions were identified.

These avoidance actions have a relatively high payback value, because many will allow you to avoid recovery costs just to restore your enterprise from a setback—resources saved and available for making real progress toward your goals.

Other possibilities may be helpful.

Risk	Avoidance Actions
Extended electrical outage	Keep trees near above-ground power lines trimmed
HVAC experiences unscheduled downtime	Maintain an onsite inventory of critical spare parts
Injury accident on premises	Pressure wash approaches to entrances once per year
Ice or sleet makes entrances slippery and dangerous	Keep a supply of sand on premises
Project slippage	Establish project management standards
Interruption in USPS delivery of client payments	Reduce reliance on USPS for client payments
Investment risks	Diversify holdings
Grant is canceled	Identify additional sources of funding
Excessive delays in receiving approval to proceed	Establish an agreement on the time limit for critical decisions
Data recovery does not work properly	Test data recovery process monthly

Exercise #3: Identify actions that can avoid or significantly reduce the possibility of your risks from becoming real.

(Stop! Do it!)

This is a good time to assess where you are in learning the Protect-Biz risk management planning process and in reflecting on the value it provides. If you have attempted the exercises, you now have a list of some potential obstacles between you and your goals. These possibilities are now located in your foresight and thus cannot catch you totally by surprise unless you deliberately forget or ignore them. This is value. What you do with this new foresight is up to you. The remaining steps of the Protect-Biz risk management planning process will guide you in completing your plan for these risks, and that will provide additional value.

6. How to Anticipate (Part 1) —Trip Wires and Trip Wire Monitors (Knowing When Action Is Needed)

> Our eyes only see the big dimensions, but beyond those there are others that escape detection because they are so small.
>
> —Brian Greene, scientist and author

When the results from your marketing and sales efforts slow down, you take action. When your manufacturing processes create products that are out of tolerance, you take action. When a project is running over the budget and the planned schedule, you take action. This is a tried-and-true principle of effective management. Why then is it not applied universally across all activities that are designed to achieve your goals? The actions would be the same: define tolerance criteria, monitor the process, and take action when the tolerances are exceeded. These additional specified tolerances are just as important in creating and maintaining a sustainable enterprise.

The world is replete with problems that could have been detected much earlier than they actually were. Market changes, maintenance problems, personnel issues, neighborhood crime trends, increasing delays in customer payments, even student pilots who have no interest in learning how to land an aircraft can sneak up on us as they grow into larger and more costly problems to solve. These can threaten your enterprise just as much as missed monthly sales targets.

> ### *Definitions: Trip Wire and Trip Wire Monitor*
> Trip wire: objective criteria for identifying the need to take action; evidence that the risk has become a real obstacle. Trip wire monitor: who, by name, title, or role, is responsible for monitoring the trip wire and then alerting those who have the authority to approve actions to mitigate risks that have become real.

The Protect-Biz risk management planning process helps you detect growing problems with the use of trip wires. A trip wire is a specific and objective criterion that alerts you to the fact that action is required because a potential obstacle is becoming real. While defining trip wires is not the easiest step in the Protect-Biz risk management planning process, it is most certainly very powerful. And it is not commonly found in other risk management planning processes.

> ### Case Study
>
> Think back to what happened to the Superdome in Louisiana in the aftermath of Hurricane Katrina—the interior suffered extensive damage beyond that caused by the storm itself. This experience offers an example of the need for trip wires. The risk of lawlessness in such confined, stressful, and overpacked circumstances should be a risk identified in any plan for an evacuation shelter. A trip wire could have been defined as the maximum ratio of evacuees to security personnel—maybe seventy-five to one (but the specific ratio can and should be defined by law enforcement experts). The point is that if the number of security people is known and the number of evacuees is tabulated with each registration, the point at which this risk becomes real can be detected and acted upon. Once the ratio exceeds the agreed seventy-five-to-one criterion, actions to mitigate the risk should then be taken. In this case, increased security personnel added earlier may have had a positive effect on the eventual outcome.

Defined trip wires also allow you to delegate responsibilities in your risk management plan. Trip wire monitors are those who are in a position to first see the growing problem and first detect that a trip wire has been crossed. This powerful element of the Protect-Biz risk management planning process allows you to gain the help of others in and even outside of your enterprise in protecting your ability to achieve the goals that are important to them as well.

In the case of the Superdome, the person responsible for evacuee registrations could have been the first person to see that the registrations were approaching and would cross the defined trip wire. While he or she might not have had the authority to take action to address the problem, he or she could have had the responsibility to inform whoever did have that authority. Thus, this feature of the Protect-Biz risk management planning process guides you in gaining the participation and assistance of others in your management of risks to the enterprise—you do not need to do it alone.

Here are some examples:

Risk	Trip Wire	Trip Wire Monitor
Supplier cost increase	Greater than 3 percent increase during a six-month period	Purchasing manager
Preventive maintenance delayed	Preventive maintenance tasks delayed more than thirty days	Facilities manager
Real estate market declines	Decline of average sales price for two consecutive months	Real estate broker
Advisory firm not aligned with client objectives	Client communicates inconsistent priorities	Client advisor
Political unrest in local country	Escalating lawlessness directed at government	Local manager, government affairs department

Board governance is lax	Three or more board meetings canceled during twelve-month period	Executive director
Laboratory methods are not verifiable	Laboratory refused to adequately explain methods	Lead investigator
Inability to fill open staff positions	Less than X qualified responses to advertised positions	Human resources department
Supplier delays	Supplier misses agreed schedule	Purchasing department
Portable assets disappear	Losses exceed X dollar value per year	Asset manager
Inadequate volunteers for scheduled events	Less than needed volunteer commitments by X days before the event	Volunteer coordinator

Notice the different roles listed in the right column above. This list represents the assistance for managing risks by many others in the organization. While these sample risks were selected as sample trip wires and trip wire monitors from a number of different types of organizations, hopefully you can see how the list for one organization could have multiple trip wire monitoring assignments given to many individuals (by name, title, or role) within the organization and even outside of it, such as bookkeeper, security guard, publicist, and so on. This is clear evidence of how the Protect-Biz® risk management planning process helps you enlist the help of others in managing your risks.

If you have concluded that the Protect-Biz risk management planning process shortens the leash on your management responsibilities, you are correct. Isn't that a good thing when achieving your goals is at risk? And in doing so, it enlists the help of others by explicitly assigning responsibilities for detecting the growing problems that might go unnoticed before they reach critical mass or gain the attention of those higher in the organization.

The concept of trip wires and trip wire monitors is not commonly found in risk management planning regimens. While you may say that these elements are implied by any planning process, recall the famous statement by Will Rogers, American humorist and social commentator: "The trouble with common sense is that it isn't all that common."

Exercise #4: For each of your listed risks, define one or more trip wires that will alert you to the need to take action to minimize the impact of the risk.

(Do this one too!)

7. How to Anticipate (Part 2) —Actions to Mitigate and Authority to Mitigate

By failing to prepare, you are preparing to fail.

—Benjamin Franklin

You have now come to the final elements of your risk management plan—preplanned actions to mitigate risks that have turned into real problems. Often, this is called contingency planning (i.e., the proverbial plan B). This is the obvious element required in any risk management plan. The benefit in documenting these preplanned actions is to communicate them to others who may be required to perform these actions and to specify exactly who has the authority to authorize them. Unlike the avoidance step where your goals remain untouched, actions to mitigate may require changing your goals.

Definition: Mitigation Actions
Actions designed to reduce the impact of a risk that has become a real obstacle.

While General Eisenhower said that he found plans to be useless in battle, he asserted that the planning was indispensable. In other words, the thinking that created the plans is of critical importance. The consideration of various contingencies while in the planning mode is almost certainly more complete and effective than reactions conceived on the spot during a time of urgency and possibly confusion. Moreover, while the circumstance may not unfold exactly as planned, the advance thinking allows your Team to adjust your actions based upon the preplanning that provided a framework and most probably at least part of the actions to take. It is usually easier to adjust than to think about what to do from a blank sheet of paper, especially in urgent circumstances.

The preplanned actions often cause this plan to become confidential to the enterprise. For example, it is obvious that an enterprise would monitor the risk of clients or customers not paying your invoice. However, the actions you plan to take if this happens are probably something you want to keep to yourselves.

Definition: Authority to Mitigate
Who, by name, title, or role, has the authority to approve actions to mitigate the risk once it has occurred.

The designation of who has the authority to approve taking the actions to mitigate is important, especially if the actions incur an expense, affect relations with outside entities, or impact internal operations. This explicit designation can be by name, title, or role.

The actions to mitigate are typically very unique to the enterprise. The examples below are included here to illustrate the range of possibilities.

Risk	Actions to Mitigate	Authority to Mitigate
Cyber breach of bank accounts	Change password for online access; review incident and status with bank representatives	CFO
Key supplier goes out of business	Identify alternate suppliers; conduct due diligence, and select new supplier(s); establish purchasing agreement	Purchasing manager

Preventive maintenance falls behind schedule	Establish plan to catch up	Facilities manager
Injury accident on premises	Call 9-1-1; provide first aid if needed; assemble information for accident report; identify any witnesses, notify general manager; contact insurance agent	Building manager
Toxic spill on premises	Notify authorities, and provide information and requested support; isolate affected area; announce to building occupants; evacuate building if instructed to do so by authorities	Facilities manager
Client does not pay invoice	Offer payment options	Account manager
Unable to fill staff positions	Utilize additional media for advertising available positions	Human resources manager
Portable assets disappear	Increase frequency of audits	Asset manager

Notice the titles in the right column. Here again is evidence of how the Protect-Biz risk management planning process facilitates spreading responsibilities to effectively manage risks. After all, the livelihood of many people is directly tied to the ability of the enterprise to achieve its defined goals.

Exercise #5: For each of the risks you have defined in previous exercises, describe the actions you would expect to take once you recognize that the risk has become real and action needs to be taken to mitigate the effects of this problem. Also, designate who has the authority to approve the actions to mitigate by name, title, or role.

8. What Have Your Accomplished Here?

> Do not go where the path may lead, go instead where there is no path and leave a trail.
>
> —Ralph Waldo Emerson

The steps of the Protect-Biz risk management planning process have been completed for your short list of risks and assumptions. If you have studiously completed the five prescribed exercises, you have all of the elements necessary to manage these risks.

- You have identified the possible obstacles that might come between you and your goals—they are now in your foresight and will not completely surprise you unless you try very hard to forget or ignore what you have accomplished.
- You may have identified actions to take to better position your enterprise to either avoid or to minimize the possibility and/or impact of these potential obstacles, thus reducing potential costs and setbacks. These may lead your enterprise to new opportunities.
- You have identified how to recognize these issues when they are small, and you have designated others with the responsibility to watch them for you, thus preventing them from sneaking up on you unnoticed, as well as detecting them when they are easier and less costly to address.
- You have preplanned the responses necessary to mitigate the effects of these obstacles and explicitly delegated responsibility for approving the actions where possible, thus orienting your organization toward proper response.

- You have also communicated shared threats to the enterprise and the interests of everyone associated with the enterprise as a foundation for increased teamwork.

While the plan created by these exercises has been limited to a small number of risks, you can use your new knowledge to add more risks and develop a more complete plan.

The contents of this risk management plan do not really need a lot of verbiage surrounding them. The existing content is action oriented and easy to review and revise. The format that is produced by either the www.Protect-Biz.com wizard or by the Protect-Biz risk management planning workshop leaves you with a practical working document to effectively and efficiently manage your risks.

9. You Can Do This

Tell me and I forget. Teach me and I remember. Involve me and I learn.

—Benjamin Franklin

Our mantra "Identify, avoid, anticipate, and get back to work" established the themes that have shaped this process and the content of this book:

- risk management is a means to goal accomplishment, not an end into itself;
- risk management can be straightforward and economical;
- risk management can be accomplished by busy people with other things to do; and
- anyone can achieve independence and self-sufficiency in effectively managing the risks to his or her enterprise.

I believe *IF...*, *THEN...* has delivered on these promises. This process has proven itself many times. But bringing the benefits of risk management to your enterprise depends upon you.

You are now at a significant decision point in your professional career. You can either strive to incorporate risk management into your professional tool kit, or you can choose to ignore risk management, at least for the time being.

To strive to incorporate it into your tool kit requires a conscious effort, just as any new technique or tool. In this case, it is neither difficult nor time consuming. It merely requires that you take the time to complete the plan already started by the exercises in this book and schedule a small amount of time at least monthly to review your risk management plan and revise it as necessary. You will probably want to introduce risk management to some others in your organization.

You will also want to add risk management questions whenever you are reviewing proposals, recommendations, new initiatives, and operations. This part is not rocket science. Such questions as "What might go wrong?" and "What if this does not happen as planned?" will cause discussions about avoiding and anticipating the obstacles that may arise between you and your goals. This, in and of itself, will improve the plan.

Experience will help hone your skills in doing these things. And positive results will come while setbacks will be prevented and minimized.

I encourage you to apply *IF..., THEN...* for your enterprise, large or small.

10. Epilogue

Your Future Need Not Be Full Of Surprises
blog.sms-ga.com, September 2013

In a special report from the World Future Society, *The Art of Foresight* (copyright 2009), the importance of "Preparing for a Changing World" is described in some detail. It opens with "Foresight is a secret ingredient of success, because without foresight we cannot prepare for the future." It then goes on to state, "The relation of foresight to success is often poorly understood." Let me bring this lofty goal to the real world where the rubber meets the road.

Everyone can benefit from increased foresight. Our professional responsibilities demand that we anticipate the future, and our success depends upon it. Such foresight may span a range of time from a few hours to many years into the future. And the range of possibilities may include relatively small changes and universal ones, as well, be they financial/economic, technological, the competitive landscape, the workforce, regulatory requirements... you name it. If changes to these elements can affect your world, it's best that you place them into your foresight if you can. Once they are in your foresight, you will have the power to take full advantage of them or to avoid and minimize their negative impact.

But is enhancing our foresight possible? If it is truly an art form, it cannot be planned or repeated. However, I know that foresight can be dramatically enhanced without repeatedly passing through the often painful and expensive experience and hindsight. I've seen it happen many times. The Protect-Biz risk management planning process transforms the magical art of foresight into a process that may be planned and repeated.

Do you have a methodical way to envision and anticipate the future? If not, you would surely benefit from one. But just how is this possible? Just how can we identify and anticipate the possibilities we do not expect? *The Art of Foresight* identifies twelve ways to anticipate the future. The Protect-Biz risk management planning process employs one of these—(inexpensive) brainstorming. This brainstorming is accomplished within a defined eight-step process that has been proven effective across organizations large and small, as well as in many industries. The results you can derive from this process are tailored exactly to your needs regardless of the size of your organization or the industry you serve.

So are you ready to think outside the box? If you want to dramatically reduce the surprises in your future and increase the success of your enterprise, you should learn more about the tool that allows you to peer into the future and change it for the better. The starting point is www.Protect-Biz.com.

*Reprints of *The Art of Foresight* are available free of charge by contacting me at tomo@sms-ga.com.

The Original Case Study

The Protect-Biz risk management planning process was created in 1998/99 as I was helping a multinational corporation review its plans for addressing a large project with an immovable deadline—the Year 2000 problem. The company had invested hundreds of thousands of dollars in its project plan and formed a team of fifteen people to ensure that the plan was completed on time. I was asked to review the plan with "another set of eyes."

While I could have flown into town with my green eyeshade, examined their plan, and submitted a report demonstrating how smart I was, I chose to approach this task differently. I devised the Protect-Biz risk management planning process and guided the project team through it as a workshop. At the end of the workshop, the team members had documented a risk management plan containing fifty-four risks and avoidance/anticipation actions that had not been previously documented or even seriously considered. One risk I still remember was the risk that one or more members of the project team might leave the company before January 2000—certainly a significant potential obstacle in such a critical project. The project manager guiding their Year 2000 project credited this workshop with saving millions of dollars by protecting this critical project plan.

Since that time, this process has been implemented on the Internet for the single user at www.Protect-Biz.com. For a one-time fee*, the user has access to an online wizard that offers text and video guidance, as well as examples relevant to their enterprise as he or she progresses through the individual steps of the process. A one-time consultation with the author of this process is included in the single fee. This consultation is recommended at the end of the steps for identifying risks. This experience prepares the user to carry on with his or her plan at no additional charge with a lifetime license for the process and the formats. The plan can easily be downloaded into either MS Word or MS Excel for long-term use and maintenance. Remote review and comment on the final plan is available for a reasonable fee.

* The one-time fee, currently (US) $1,200, has required lots of serious thought. On the one hand, apps on the Internet typically cost a lot less (around $50). But on the other hand, www.Protect-Biz.com is not an arcade game. The user must approach it with seriousness and commitment to gain the value from it. That is more likely to happen with a nontrivial investment. There is, moreover, a money-back guarantee until the final step is completed.

The onsite workshop format continues to be available, offered by Salt Marsh Solutions Inc. of Georgia. The workshop format is designed for teams facing common risks. The fee for the workshop is based upon the size of the enterprise in terms of employees and full-time equivalents.

As an interesting side note, public workshops have been tried. But we found that individuals in a roomful of strangers just don't like to openly discuss the risks or the avoidance/anticipation actions related to their enterprises. So without the comments and questions that add such richness to the workshop experience, these were not continued.

A few independent testimonials for Protect-Biz may be of interest.

> Finally, a management tool that ties tactical activities to the strategic plan ... the plan produced by Protect-Biz demonstrates the degree of seriousness with which entrepreneurs have considered the risks of their business plan.
>
> —Yale Brown, managing partner, Columbus Ventures LLC
>
> No one else is doing risk/contingency planning this way ... the Big 4 consulting firms approach risk management from twenty-five-thousand feet. Protect-Biz provides real value much closer to the level of daily activities.
>
> —Big 4 Risk Management Consultant, Pennsylvania
>
> Tom conceived the Protect-Biz process when the deadline would not change and nothing could go wrong. It saved my client millions of dollars.
>
> —John Allen, account manager

Protect-Biz brings to light points that might never be considered but should be evaluated to keep business running at peak efficiency.

—M. Jeffrey Martin, CPA

Of course, direct consulting and collaboration by the author of this process is also available as well as special Protect-Biz.com licensing for business advisors and higher education.

Glossary of Terms

Actions to avoid: actions to be taken to reposition the enterprise to either avoid the risk altogether or to reduce either the severity of the obstacle or the probability of the risk becoming real.

Assumptions: answers to the question, "What do I/we expect to go right?"

Authority to mitigate: who, by name, title, or role, has the authority to approve actions to mitigate the risk once it has occurred.

Mitigation actions: actions designed to reduce the impact of a risk that has become a real obstacle.

Risk: any potential obstacle between you or the enterprise and goals.

Trip wire: objective criteria for identifying the need to take action; evidence the risk has become a real obstacle.

Trip wire monitor: who, by name, title, or role, is responsible for monitoring the trip wire and then alerting those who have the authority to approve actions to mitigate risks that have become real.

About the Author

How I Wound Up in Risk Management

blog.sms-ga.com, May 2013

When I was a naval officer, the question of what might go wrong was always asked. As a systems engineer, the question of what might go wrong was a constant companion. As a team leader and project manager, the question of what might go wrong was magnified by the scope of my responsibilities and by the number of people on my team. As a management consultant, the question of what might go wrong was just the beginning—clients wanted the answers. And as a Y2K consultant, supporting risk management initiatives from the computer room to the boardroom in the face of an immovable deadline, risk management moved squarely into the center of my consciousness.

The path that has brought me to my current passion for business risk management was not a planned route; it was cobbled together over many years. My passion also developed from the belief that all enterprises can gain value from the basic principles of risk management, but the concept may be intimidating to some. I want to bring the power of risk management to entrepreneurs and managers of all industries in enterprises of all sizes.

That is why I frame the Protect-Biz process as "risk management for busy people with other things to do."

Tom O'Connor

Tom O'Connor introduced Salt Marsh Solutions Inc. and serves as its CEO and principal consultant/collaborator. He created the concept of managing from a higher level and the Protect-Biz risk management planning process. Over a forty-year career as a systems and management consultant and as a project manager, O'Connor devised and implemented business process improvement solutions for Fortune 500 companies, government agencies, and international clients. He has worked in a variety of industries, including health care, education, manufacturing, public utilities, logistics, pharmaceuticals, transportation, and financial services. O'Connor served as an officer in the US Navy in the Pacific Fleet after graduating from Auburn University with a degree in industrial engineering.

O'Connor has worked for leading companies, including Electronic Data Systems, Coopers & Lybrand Consulting, Perot Systems Corporation, KPMG ExIS, Computer Sciences Corporation, and Data Dimensions Inc.

His considerable expertise includes the following:

❖ applying successful innovation for both the sales and delivery of consulting services;
❖ establishing productivity improvement techniques and usability testing within a Fortune 100 technology company;
❖ managing client projects with budgets up to $22 million;
❖ managing a staff of three hundred systems engineers supporting multiple federal government projects;
❖ improving many consulting projects that were not meeting client expectations; and
❖ advising national and international clients on critical, time-sensitive issues that challenged the boardroom as well as the computer room.

In addition, O'Connor has authored articles for *Computerworld*, *InformationWeek*, the *e.MILE People Development Magazine*, and the *D7 Connection*, the US Coast Guard District 7 human resources quarterly publication.

"I don't just plan to make things happen; I make things happen."

Contact information:

tomo@sms-ga.com

Made in the USA
Lexington, KY
18 March 2015